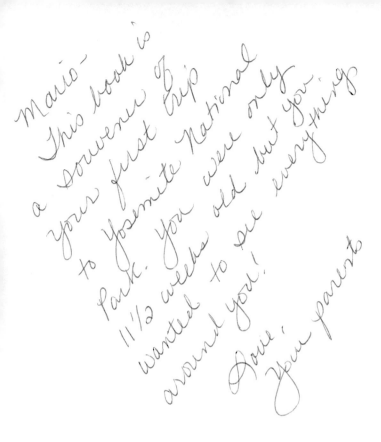

Mario—
This book is
a souvenir of
your first trip
to Yosemite National
Park. You were only
1 1/2 weeks old but you
wanted to see everything
around you!

Love,
Your parents

# HOW THE
# FOREST GREW

## by William Jaspersohn
## illustrated by Chuck Eckart

A Mulberry Paperback Book   New York

The author wishes to thank Charles W. Johnson, chief naturalist for the
Agency of Environmental Conservation, Vermont Department of Forests,
Parks, and Recreation, for reading the text of this book and offering valuable
suggestions and factual corrections.

First Mulberry Edition, 1992.            3   4   5   6   7   8   9   10

Library of Congress Cataloging in Publication Data
Jaspersohn, William.      How the forest grew.
Summary: Describes the gradual transformation of a cleared farm field into a dense forest.
1. Forest ecology—Juvenile literature.   2. Ecological succession—Juvenile Literature.
[1. Forests and forestry.   2. Forest ecology.   3. Ecology.]   I. Eckart, Chuck.   II. Title.
QH541.5.F6J37   574.5'264   79-16286   ISBN 0-688-11508-X

For
DAVID LUCE,
the healing friend,
whose own life growth
continues ceaselessly    –W.J.

For ALICE    –C.E.

Have you ever wondered
where forests come from,
and how they grow?
This book is about a hardwood
forest in Massachusetts.
It could be about a forest
anywhere because most forests
grow the same way.
To find out how
this Massachusetts forest grew,
we must go back in time.
We must see how
the forest land looked
two hundred years ago.

Two hundred years ago

the land was open and green.

But then the farmer and his family

who owned the land,

and who had cleared it,

moved away.

Changes began.

The wind blew seeds across the fields.

Birds dropped seeds from the air.

The sun warmed the seeds.

The rain watered them,

and they grew.

In a few years the land was filled

with weeds–with dandelions

and goldenrod and chickweed.

And milkweed with its pods of fluff.

And ragweed and black-eyed Susans.

Each spring new plants took root.

The land began to look different.

Burdock and briars

grew among the weeds,

making the land moist and brushy.

Blackberries grew.

Birds came to eat them—

song sparrows, bobolinks,

and catbirds.

Meadow mice
and cottontail rabbits
made their nests
in the tall grass.
Woodchucks, moles, and shrews
dug their tunnels in the ground.
Snakes came to feed
on the small animals.
Hawks and owls
hunted over the land
for their food.
Time passed.

And then one summer

five years after the farm family left,

a tree seedling sprouted.

It wasn't a cedar or a birch seedling,

or a poplar or an aspen seedling,

though it could have been

because these trees like full sunlight.

No, it was a white pine seedling,

another sun-loving tree.

The wind had blown its seed

from a nearby forest.

The seed sprouted.

That same summer
more white pine seedlings sprouted.
The land was speckled
with tiny dots of green.
Year after year,
through weeds and low brush,
the little trees pushed their way up.
Tree scientists call the first trees
that take hold on a piece of land
*pioneer trees.*
That is what these white pines were.
No other sun-loving tree
grows in such numbers,
or so fast.

As the pine trees grew,

brush-dwelling birds

moved onto the land.

They replaced the field dwellers.

Towhees, warblers, and field sparrows

made their homes in the thickets.

But so did weasels and foxes
who caught mice, rabbits, and birds
for their dinner.

Twenty years after

the first pine seedling sprouted,

the land was covered with white pines.

Their branches blocked the sun's rays.

The old weeds and grasses

died from want of light.

But what the pines did

to the old weeds,

they also did to their own kind.

When new white pine seedlings

tried to grow,

they couldn't get sunlight,

and they died.

Only those seedlings

that liked the shade

grew beneath

the stands of white pines.

Ash trees, red oak, red maple,

and tulip trees–

these were the trees

that the white pines

helped the most.

In less than fifteen years
the new trees were crowding
the white pines for space.
A struggle had begun,
only the strongest
trees would survive.
Scientists call this change
from one kind of tree or animal
to a new kind *succession*.
They say that one kind of tree
or animal succeeds another.

As the new trees on the land
began to succeed the old pines,
the animal life on the land
changed, too.
The meadow mice moved because
their food supply was gone,
and there was no more grass
for them to build their nests.
White-footed mice took their place.
They made their nests
in hollow stumps and logs.
They ate seeds
from the trees and shrubs.

For the first time

deer came to live on the land.

Now there were places

for them to hide

and tender shoots

for them to eat.

Cardinals perched in the trees.
So did redstarts,
ovenbirds, and ruffed grouse.
Squirrels and chipmunks
brought nuts onto the land.
Some of these sprouted
with the other seedlings.

Forty years had passed since

the farmer and his family had left.

And then one summer afternoon,

fifty years after the farm family had gone,

a storm broke over the land.

Lightning struck the tallest pines,

killing some of them

and damaging others.

Strong winds uprooted more pines,

and lightning fires scorched branches.

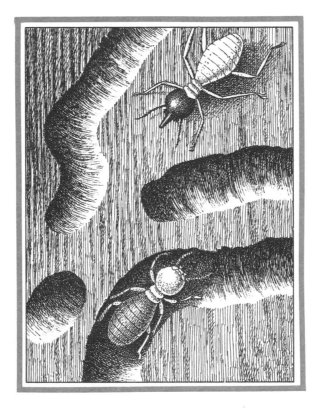

But this is how forests grow.

The death of some of the pine trees

made room for new and different trees

that had been sprouting

on the forest floor.

As time passed, insects and disease

hurt the other pines.

Every time one of them died,

a red oak, white ash,

or red maple tree

took its place.

The forest grew.

By the year 1860,

more than eighty years

after the farm family had left,

the weeds were all gone.

The pioneer white pines

were nearly all gone.

Red oaks, red maples,

and ash trees were everywhere.

The forest had reached

its *middle stage.*

Now on the forest floor

came the last of the new seedlings.

These were the beeches

and the sugar maples,

trees that like the deep shade.

The other seedlings—

the red oak, red maple,

and ash seedlings—needed more light.

And some of them needed more water,

and different kinds of soil to grow in.

So they died, and the beech

and the sugar maple seedlings

took their place.

Every autumn

the trees lost their leaves.

They fell to the ground

with dead twigs and branches.

All of these things decayed

and made a rich layer of stuff

called *humus.*

Then slowly,

bacteria, worms, and fungi

turned the humus into soil

from which the trees

got food and water.

Sometimes an animal

or an insect died, and its body

became part of the humus, too.

One hundred years had passed
since the farm family had moved.
Now, whenever a red oak, red maple,
or white ash tree died, it made room for
the smaller beeches and sugar maples.
These formed a layer below the older trees
called an *understory*.

Every winter, snow blanketed
the forest floor.
Every spring, the ground
was covered with wildflowers.
Year after year,
the beeches and sugar maple trees
pushed their branches toward the sky.
Hemlocks grew in their shade.
Slowly, one by one,
most of the red oak, red maple,
and ash trees disappeared.

By the year 1927,

which was one hundred and fifty years

after the forest had begun,

the beeches and sugar maples

were the kings of the forest.

Today a family owns the land

and they love the peaceful forest.

They build their house on the same spot

where the farm family once built theirs.

But they do not clear

the land this time.

Instead, they listen and look.

What was once open fields

is now a magnificent forest.

It is home for many wild animals—

for foxes, bobcats, wood turtles,

chipmunks, bears, deer, squirrels,

mice, porcupines,

and many other creatures.

Its tree roots hold water
and keep the soil from washing away.
Birds of many kinds
nest in its branches.
Its humus enriches the earth's soil.
All through the world
other forests are growing
like the one in Massachusetts.
The kinds of trees in each forest
may be different, but the way they
grow is very much the same.
Nothing in a forest ever stands still.
Old trees are dying and making room
for new trees every day.

# THE NEXT TIME
# YOU GO
# INTO A FOREST:

Think how long it took to grow.

Try and learn the names
of the different trees.

Most forests
have three stages of growth:
  🌿 the pioneer stage
  🌿 the middle stage
  🌿 the final, or climax stage
See if you can tell which stage
of growth the forest is in.

52

A full-grown forest has five layers:

- the canopy
- the understory
- the shrub layer
- the herbal layer
- the forest floor layer.

Can you find all five?

If you find a tree stump
and count its growth rings,
you will know the tree's age.

Fungi live on rotting
trees and plants.
Look for them on fallen
logs and stumps.

Can you find signs of insects
that have hurt trees?
Can you find signs of woodpeckers?

Know the different signs
of animal life in a forest:

- tracks
- scat
- feathers, fur, or snakeskins
- nests, burrows, dens
- bones, skeletons

Do you know the poisonous plants
in a forest?

- poison ivy
- poison oak
- poison sumac